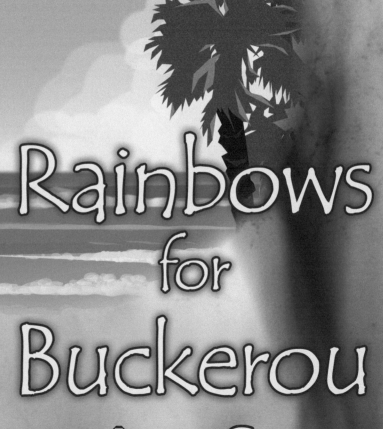

Rainbows
for
Buckerou

RICK FLEURY AND LINDA STAEHR
ILLUSTRATOR TREVOR PRESLEY

WestBow Press books may be ordered through booksellers or by contacting:

WestBow Press
A Division of Thomas Nelson
1663 Liberty Drive
Bloomington, IN 47403
www.westbowpress.com
1-(866) 928-1240

Because of the dynamic nature of the Internet, any web addresses or links contained in this book may have changed since publication and may no longer be valid. The views expressed in this work are solely those of the author and do not necessarily reflect the views of the publisher, and the publisher hereby disclaims any responsibility for them.

Any people depicted in stock imagery provided by Thinkstock are models, and such images are being used for illustrative purposes only.

Certain stock imagery ® Thinkstock.

ISBN: 978-1-4497-8775-2 (sc)
ISBN: 978-1-4497-8761-5 (e)

Library of Congress Control Number: 2013904521

Printed in the United States of America

WestBow Press rev. date: 06/14/2019

WESTBOW
PRESS®
A DIVISION OF THOMAS NELSON
& ZONDERVAN

To Mom and Brother Bob

When I was 11 years old I
had to leave my family.
They didn't have time for me,
I was lonely.
So one morning I went
out into the world.
I always liked the beach,
so I headed there.

It was a great day!
A cool breeze pushing up my fur,
the smell of fish from the ocean,
and lots of sunshine to keep me warm.
Oh, there's a rooftop where
I can watch the birds!

Look! I see a man on that balcony.
I wonder if he has any food.
I went up to him.
I guess I looked hungry.
He did have food!

This nice man likes to feed me.
I guess I found a new home!
Every time he says "Buckerou"
he looks at me,
so I guess that is my new name.
Every time people say "Rick"
they look at him;
I guess that is his name.
Rick likes to surf the ocean waves,
which I can see from my balcony.
He surfs near a spot in the water where
you can see a large rock at low tide.
I like to watch.

I love to be with Rick and his
friends on the balcony.
He tells them about meeting people
on the pier near here, where he
tells the people about Jesus.
It's great here all year round.
I watch my area outside, so
no other cat takes over.

Sometimes I get to follow the sun's
rays on the balcony, or on the roof.
When it is cold I get to lie
in the apartment with Rick
in front of the heater.
But my favorite time is listening
to the ocean at night.

Rick told me it has been 13 years
since I came to live with him,
we have become the best of friends.
But I think my body is wearing out, so
I purr more these days to feel good.
I am so skinny now,
I have trouble staying on the
roof on a windy day.
This morning when I jumped through
my window as I always do,
I felt like my whole body broke.
Rick took me to a doctor to
see what was wrong.
The doctor said she was sorry
but she couldn't fix me.
Then Rick told me I had to go now.

Buckerou did go that day and
Rick really missed Buckerou.
He felt terrible; he knew this was
going to be a very sad time.
He came home to an empty house
and it seemed lonely there.
However God was there to comfort him.
One week after his last day with Buck,
Rick went out on the balcony.
Seeing the rock, he decided Buck's
ashes should be scattered there.
Rick remembered that The
Rock is sometimes another
name for Jesus in the Bible.
At that moment he saw a rainbow
appear over the ocean.
The rainbow ended at that very rock!
Rick had never seen a
rainbow there before.

Rick thought of how God made a promise
thousands of years ago about a rainbow.
As he admired the beautiful rainbow Rick wondered,
could God want to remind me that whenever
a rainbow appears in the clouds,
I will see it and remember the everlasting promise between God
and all living creatures of every kind on the earth?

Weeks later when Rick was on the balcony again,
another rainbow appeared at the very same spot.
For it to be there twice God must be reminding
Rick of His promise through this rainbow.

Now Rick had Buckerou's ashes in a box.
He opened the box and a story with "Rainbow
Bridge" written at the top was inside.
It told about how our pets wait for us in heaven.
Rick believes there are animals in heaven because the
Bible talks about them. Then Rick and his friend took
the ashes to the beach. There they kneeled on the sand,
said their prayers and thanked God for Buckerou.

Next Rick and his friend put the box on his
surfboard and paddled out to the rock.
A dolphin suddenly poked his head up and looked right at Rick.
After the dolphin swam away
Rick wondered if maybe God was showing the
dolphin that God's friends never die.

Rick looked toward the pier.
He was amazed to see small perfect rainbows of
every color appearing on each breaking wave.
With tears, Rick then scattered Buckerou's ashes into the water.

Now as Rick watches the sunset he sees
the fishermen,
the surfers,
and the other people enjoying
His creation at the beach.
He is reminded how special
we are to God.
Rick knows that God loves him, to have
given him Buckerou all those years.
Everything is going to be all right,
Yes, God will make sure everything
is going to be all right.

Rainbow Bridge

There is a bridge connecting Heaven and Earth, it is
called Rainbow Bridge because of it's many colors.
Just this side of Rainbow Bridge there is a land of
meadows,hills and valleys with lush green grass.

When a beloved pet dies, the pet goes to this place. There
is always food and water and warm Spring weather.
The old and frail animals are young again. Those
who are maimed are made whole again.
They play all day with each other.

There is only one thing missing. They are not with their
special person who loved them on Earth. So each day
they run and play until the day comes when
one suddenly stops playing and looks up!
The nose twitches! The ears are up! The eyes are
staring! And this one suddenly runs from the group!

You have been seen,and when you and your special friend
meet,you take him or her in your arms and embrace.
Your face is kissed again and again,and you
look into tne eyes of your trusting pet.

When you cross the Rainbow Bridge
together,never to be seperated again.

Author Unknown

Perhaps you are a bit like Buckerou in Rick's story… And maybe you are without a place to call home. You know you need a change and a new start. Buckerou found his home with a loving master, who gave him peace and comfort.

Jesus has provided a new home in Heaven for those that trust in Him, and it lasts for eternity. Jesus loves you so much that He hung on a cross to pay the penalty for sin (the things we do that we know are wrong). These sins will keep anyone from going to Heaven, and what you need to do is ask God for forgiveness, and trust in what Jesus did on the cross. Here are some Bible verses that explain how to ask for forgiveness:

"For God so loved the world, that He gave his only begotten Son, that whoever believes in Him should not perish but have everlasting life." (John 3:16)

God also said "that if you confess with your mouth
the Lord Jesus and believe in your heart that God has
raised him from the dead you will be saved…"

"…For with the heart one believes to righteousness, and with the
mouth confession is made unto salvation." (Romans 10:9-10)

If you want to trust in Jesus, but don't know
what to say, here is a prayer you can pray:

"God, I know that I am a sinner, and Jesus died on the cross
for my sins. Thank you for dying in my place, I now ask you
into my heart as Lord and Savior. I will do my best to follow
Jesus, and turn from my sins, for the rest of my life."

If you have trusted in Jesus in your heart, God will forgive you,
and you will spend eternity in Heaven with Jesus, God Bless.

Printed in the United States
By Bookmasters